# CALIFORNIA GOLD RUSH:
## A Letter Home

### by Catherine Quirin

Editorial Offices: Glenview, Illinois • Parsippany, New Jersey • New York, New York
Sales Offices: Needham, Massachusetts • Duluth, Georgia • Glenview, Illinois
Coppell, Texas • Ontario, California • Mesa, Arizona

Every effort has been made to secure permission and provide appropriate credit for photographic material. The publisher deeply regrets any omission and pledges to correct errors called to its attention in subsequent editions.

Unless otherwise acknowledged, all photographs are the property of Scott Foresman, a division of Pearson Education.

Photo locators denoted as follows: Top (T), Center (C), Bottom (B), Left (L), Right (R), Background (Bkgd)

Opener: Getty Royalty Free, Denver Public Library; 3 Richard Stergulz; 4 Library of Congress; 5 Library of Congress; 6 Library of Congress; 7 ©Comstock; 8 Library of Congress; 9 ©Comstock, Denver Public Library; 10 Getty Images; 11 Richard Stergulz; 12 Denver Public Library

ISBN: 0-328-13322-1

Copyright © Pearson Education, Inc.

All Rights Reserved. Printed in the United States of America. This publication is protected by Copyright, and permission should be obtained from the publisher prior to any prohibited reproduction, storage in a retrieval system, or transmission in any form by any means, electronic, mechanical, photocopying, recording, or likewise. For information regarding permission(s), write to: Permissions Department, Scott Foresman, 1900 East Lake Avenue, Glenview, Illinois 60025.

7 8 9 10 V0G1 14 13 12 11 10 09 08

Josh rushed through the doorway. "Ma! Pa!" he yelled. "I've fetched a letter from Uncle Zach. He's looking for gold in California!"

"Read the letter, Pa," said Ma.

Pa started to read. Josh wanted to hear all about life in the California gold fields.

*October 1850*

*Dear Family,*

*I met two men named Matthew and Peter while on the trail going west. We became friends. We decided to travel together for safety. Our trip was long. We were mighty happy to cross the mountains into California!*

Gold seekers crossing the mountains

*We claimed a spot along the American River. Then we went into San Francisco to buy tools to pan for gold.*

*San Francisco is a busy boom town! New houses are being built. Businesses are opening everywhere we look. There are people here from all around the world.*

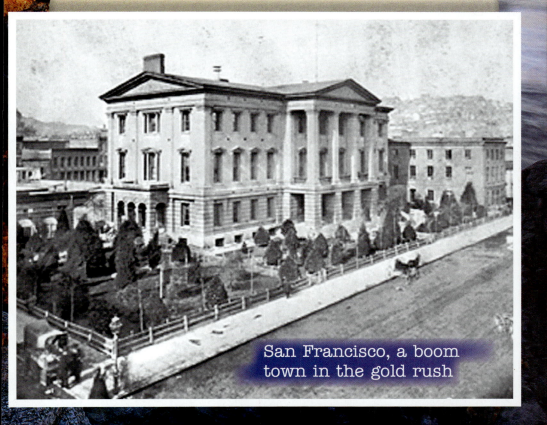

San Francisco, a boom town in the gold rush

*We each bought a pick, a shovel, and some pans. This cost us most of our coins. We set up tents in a mining town near our claim. Some miners don't even have a tent. They have to sleep on the ground.*

Tents and shelters in a mining town

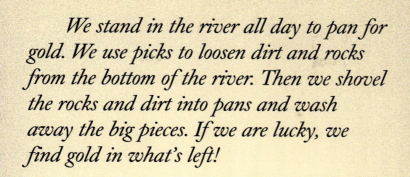

We stand in the river all day to pan for gold. We use picks to loosen dirt and rocks from the bottom of the river. Then we shovel the rocks and dirt into pans and wash away the big pieces. If we are lucky, we find gold in what's left!

Miners sifting through dirt, hoping to find gold

We had no luck at all until we bought a gold cradle. To work the cradle, one person shovels rocks and dirt into it while another rocks the cradle back and forth. Water is poured over the dirt. Finer sand and gold are washed through a screen and trapped on the floor of the cradle.

A gold cradle

*On Sundays all the miners take a rest. Many men write letters home. Sunday is also a good day to do laundry and mending. I sure miss the food at home! Here we cook salt pork in a skillet over an open fire.*

A group of miners in California

*I'm sure you're wondering if we've had any big gold strikes. We haven't. In the spring our group will split up. Matthew is going to stay. Peter and I will head home.*

*See you in the spring,*

*Zach*

Workers at a mine

Pa finished reading the letter. Everyone sat quietly. Josh had been hoping to join his uncle for an adventure in California. Now he couldn't wait for Zach to come home.

# The Gold Rush

About eighty thousand miners arrived in California in 1849. Because of this, they were nicknamed the "'49ers." At the very beginning of the gold rush, gold was easy to find. It could be panned right out of the rivers. This gold was called surface gold. All the miners needed were a pick and a pan. Sometimes all they had to do was look down into the water to find a very shiny nugget!

As more people came to hunt for gold, the surface gold was claimed. That meant that the miners had to work harder to find gold. Some began to work together with equipment such as the cradle, or rocker.

The California Gold Rush lasted about ten years.